بسم الله الرحمن الرحيم

Bismi Llahi r-Rahmani r-Rahim

In the Name of Allah the Most Kind, the Most Caring.

"When you are greeted with a greeting, reply with one better than it or return it. Allah keeps account of all things."
(4:86)

Other Titles By This Author:

My Little Lore of Light
The Light of Muhammad
Links of Light: The Golden Chain
The Story of Moses
Who Are You? A Book of Very Serious Questions
The Animals of Paradise
The Animals of Paradise: Coloring Book
My Little Lore of Light: Coloring Book
Every Day A Thousand Times
Ibrahim Khalil Allah
As-Salamu 'Alaykum Ya Rasul Allah (sas)

With love to Mawlana Shaykh Nazim al-Haqqani

and Hajjah Anne.

And to Haniya, Humayra, Layka, Ishaq, Jacob, Hamza, Ghalib, Khalil, Noura, Karima, Tarik, Hala, and all the little people of paradise.

Printed in the United States of America ISBN 978-0-9913003-8-9
Little Bird Books littlebirdbooksink@gmail.com

Animal Salams

By

Karima Sperling

"As-salamu 'alaykum Mr. Owl" say I.
"Hoo—loo to-woo" is his hooted reply.

"As-salamu 'alaykum Mrs. Cat" say I.

"Good Meow-ning to you" is her purring reply.

"As-salamu 'alaykum Mr. Dog" say I.

"Bow wow-nderful day" is his panted reply.

"As-salamu 'alaykum Mrs. Cow" say I.

"Good after-mooo-n to you" is her lowing reply.

"As-salamu 'alaykum Mr. Sheep" say I.

"Baaa bye to you" is his bleated reply.

"As-salamu 'alaykum Ms. Mouse" say I.

"Good Eee-vening to you" is her squeaky reply.

"As-salamu 'alaykum Mr. Horse" say I.

"And a Good neigh-t to you" is his whinnied reply.

"As-Salamu 'alaykum Miss Dove" say I.

"Tweet dreams to you" is her cooing reply.

But when you say "As-salamu 'alaykum" to me, I say to you...

"Wa 'alaykum as-salam
wa rahmatu Llahi wa barakatuhu!"

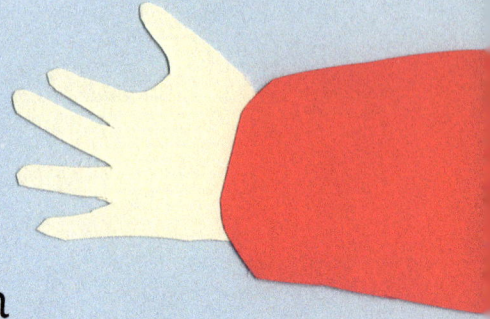

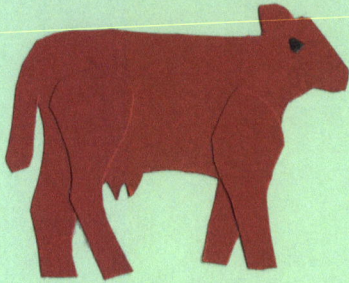

As-salaa – **moo**

'a-**neigh**

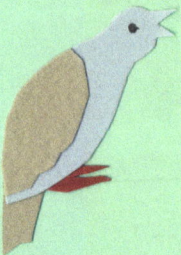

coo-m

wa rah-**maa**-tu

Allah -*eeee*

wa **bar(k)**

a- **cat**

to-**hoooo**

The End

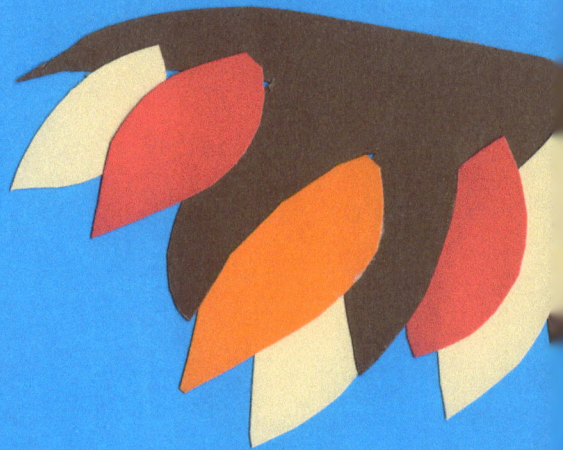

www.ingramcontent.com/pod-product-compliance
Lightning Source LLC
Chambersburg PA
CBHW042118040426
42449CB00002B/92